Rocket Fuel

Take Your Relationship With God To A Higher Level

Jacob Schmelzer

Rocket Fuel

DEDICATION

To my wonderful wife Bethany and our amazing children.
To Follow Student Ministries. To the three men who
shaped my devotional life more than anyone else: my dad
Steve, my intern director John, and my pastor, Gary.

CONTENTS

Rocket Fuel

Intro

As goes the fuel so goes the fire. This is true of planes, trains, and automobiles and it's true of you and me. What we fuel our lives with determines how high we can fly. Rocket Fuel is about filling your life with the Spirit and the Word of God so that you can achieve the heights He has destined for you. Interestingly, as technologically complex as a rocket is, it can only fulfill its purpose if it is properly fueled. All that designed power and fury will sit still as stone without fuel. We are the same. To achieve the atmosphere breaking power that God created us for we must connect with our power source, God Himself.

Rocket Fuel is about learning how to properly fuel your life. As followers of Christ we have been called to love God with all of our heart, soul, mind, and strength and to love our neighbors as ourselves. While that may sound simple in theory, it is incredibly challenging in practice. Like so many aspiring dreamers who desperately worked to break free from earth's atmosphere to reach outer space we aspire to the heights of our destiny in Christ. As a rocket's fuel allows it to achieve enough lift to overcome gravity our fuel aids us in our struggle to overcome the gravitational pull of pride, power, and possessions.

As Peter wrote,

> *"By his divine power, God has given us everything we need for living a godly life..."* (2 Peter 1:3a NLT)

God has given us EVERYTHING we need for living a godly life! When I read these words I am encouraged that I can live the life that God has called me to. God has given me everything I need. But how does this happen? How can we do it? The secret is found in the second part of the verse. Peter continues,

"We have received all of this by coming to know him, the one who called us to himself by means of his marvelous glory and excellence." (2 Peter 1:3b NLT)

We receive everything we need by coming to know Christ! He is the one who has called us to Himself. A relationship with Jesus is the Rocket Fuel.

Let these words sink into your heart and mind: WITH CHRIST. With Christ you can be all He's destined you to be. With Christ you can do all He's called you to do. With Christ you are more than a conqueror. Without Christ you'll fall flat. You'll never be able to break out of the atmosphere of your own limitations. So many people believe that they have what it takes inside of themselves but find out later they were sorely mistaken. Only through Christ can you overcome your weaknesses and become the person that God intended you to be all along.

Jacob Schmelzer

Chapter 1

A few years ago I had a conversation with a lady who had been a Christian for several years. She wanted to become a member at our church and I was conducting an interview to help her take that step. During our conversation I casually mentioned my daily "devotions" and she said, "What does that mean?" I paused for a moment and then responded, "You know...devotions? Quiet time? Time with God?" The blank stare I got in return let me know my lingo wasn't quite connecting. I told her that as a Christian I tried to spend time with God every day by reading my Bible and praying. She responded with a statement that stopped me in my tracks.

"That sounds nice but I can't do that."

I just waited, not knowing what to say.

She continued, "I don't know how to pray. I don't know what to say."

For a moment I was speechless but then I launched in and did my best to give a short lesson on what prayer was and how to do it. She nodded politely but I could tell I wasn't doing very well. I was caught flat-footed. Here was someone who was interested in becoming a member of the church and was a self-confessed follower of Christ. And yet, she didn't know how to pray. She hadn't been taught the value of devotions, or even what they were, but she had a sincere desire to have a relationship with Christ.

It hit me. There was a need here. Why should any follower of Christ struggle with the idea of relating to God? I'd been taught from a young age about devotions. My parents modeled the disciplines of prayer and Bible reading. I'd been taught in kids church that a daily time with God was vital to my faith and was shown how to read my Bible and pray. These were fundamental practices to me but they were foreign to the lady I was talking to. What made it worse was that somewhere on her journey she'd picked up the idea that prayer and relationship with God were difficult and confusing. She had the idea that prayer was a ritual that had to be performed correctly or not at all. She was held captive by a thought that simply wasn't true.

Relationship with God isn't a matter of performing elaborate rituals or saying certain words. The entire basis of our relationship with God is accepting what Christ did for us at the cross. It's a passive acceptance of God's mercy and an active response of repentance in return. John, one of Jesus' disciples, wrote,

> *"We love Him because He first loved us."*
> (1 John 4:19 NKJV)

We love Him because He first loved us! My relationship with God always starts with His love for me. I don't pray or read my Bible to earn God's favor. I do those things to experience and enjoy His friendship! Devotions are not meant to separate the un-informed from God's presence. They are an opportunity for everyone to access His presence and to enjoy fellowship with Him. Reading the Bible teaches us about God's character and nature. It reveals to us His justice and His mercy. It tells us the true story of reality, of creation, the fall, our redemption, and God's final victory.

Simply, prayer is talking to God. Prayer allows us to communicate with Him. It allows us to hear His voice, receive His direction and follow His leading. In prayer, God also hears us. We can tell Him of our needs and confess our weaknesses. We can pour out our worship as an offering to the Father who is a constant presence of strength and love in our lives. Prayer shouldn't be approached as a ritual but rather as a conversation.

The simple disciplines of prayer and Bible study can lead us into a rich and satisfying relationship with God. They are well-worn pathways that have led seekers throughout history to incredible encounters with God. One such seeker was the great reformer, Martin Luther, who while reading the book of Romans came to his amazing insight of salvation by grace through faith. That revelation reformed the church but it was the simple act of reading the scriptures that reformed his heart.

Jacob Schmelzer

Chapter 2

Why Devotions?

Before we get into the "how" it's important we look at the "why." The "why" of devotions is found in the person and work of Jesus Christ. Jesus restored the possibility of relationship with God the Father! Most believers have at least a basic understanding that Jesus died to pay for their sins and give them eternal life but they may miss this incredibly rich truth. Jesus' sacrifice opened up access to God's presence right now!

Dallas Willard said it like this, "The gospel isn't how to get to heaven after you die. The gospel is how to get to heaven before you die." Jesus' work at the cross opened up an entirely new way of life to us! We no longer have to live separated and alone. We can have a rich relationship with God. What sin stole, Jesus has restored. Adam and Eve walked and talked with God in the garden but were cut off because of their sin. Now through Jesus we can connect with our creator once more!

This is the stunning invitation that a devotional life offers us. "Come and spend time with the creator of heaven and earth! Talk with the author of life! Let your soul rest in the arms of the Father. Come and know your purpose and destiny! Enjoy fellowship with God your Father!"

Approaching God

It is my belief that a daily habit of devotions is one of the best practices that a Christian can have. But, many believers neglect this amazing opportunity. Do they not understand what is being offered? Listen to these words from the writer of Hebrews,

"14 So then, since we have a great High Priest who has entered heaven, Jesus the Son of God, let us hold firmly to what we believe. 15 This High Priest of ours understands our weaknesses, for he faced all of the same testings we do, yet he did not sin. 16 So let us come boldly to the throne of our gracious God. There we will receive his mercy, and we will find grace to help us when we need it most."
(Hebrews 4:14–16 NLT)

We have been offered free access to the throne room of God! Let's put it in different terms to make it clearer. Imagine that the president of the United States installed a secret door that allowed you access into the oval office and gave you the key. Then imagine that he said you could come in anytime day or night and ask him for whatever you needed. What if you had that kind of access? That's a little simplistic because the kind of access we've been offered to God through Christ is so much greater!

Jacob Schmelzer

Through Jesus we've literally been invited into the presence of the Creator of the Universe! It's one of the greatest benefits of faith in Christ. It's the restoration of what God created us for and established in the garden of Eden.

I love that line, "So let us come boldly to the throne of our gracious God." This describes the attitude and posture of how we are to approach God. We should come boldly to receive His mercy and grace when we need it most. How is this possible? It's because Jesus is our High Priest. In the Old Testament the high priest would "go between" God and the people and this is what Jesus does for us. His sacrifice once and for all paid the price for our sin and reconciled us with God. Jesus is the door to relationship with God for now and all eternity!

So how does this work practically? Obviously there isn't a physical location where we approach God's throne. Prayer is the way we approach God's throne. Listen to how

Charles Spurgeon describes prayer as an approach,

> *"True prayer is an approach of the soul by the Spirit of God to the throne of God. It is not the utterance of words, it is not alone the feeling of desires, but it is the advance of the desires to God, the spiritual approach of our nature towards the Lord our God. True prayer is not a mere mental exercise, nor a vocal performance, but it is deeper far than that—it is spiritual commerce with the Creator of heaven and earth."* (C. H. Spurgeon "Sermon on The Throne of Grace")

I love what he said about how prayer is far deeper than words and feelings. Prayer is the advance of our desires to God, "the spiritual approach of our nature towards the Lord our God." Prayer is not a magic formula or secret combination of words. It is a spiritual posture of approach towards God. It is the natural response of a heart that has received the truth and power of the Gospel! When I truly believe that I have been made right with God by faith in Christ I will come boldly to God's throne in prayer.

We also approach God through reading the Bible. The Bible is God's presentation to mankind of who He is, what He's done, and what He's going to do. Francis Schaeffer said this about the Bible,

> *"First, the Bible tells men and women true things about God. Therefore, they can know true things about God. One can know true things about God because God has revealed Himself...And the Bible speaks to men and women concerning meaning, morals, and values. Second, the Bible tells us true things about people and about nature. It does not give men and women exhaustive truth about the world and the cosmos, but it does give truth about them. So one can know many*

true things about nature, especially why things exist and why they have the form they have. Yet, because the Bible does not give exhaustive truth about history and the cosmos, historians and scientists have a job to do, and their work is not meaningless. To be sure, there is a total break between God and His creation, that is, between God and created things; God is infinite and created things are finite. But man can know both truth about God and truth about the things of creation because in the Bible God has revealed Himself and has given man the key to understanding God's world."

The Bible gives us an incredible basis of truth upon which to construct our lives. It reveals truth about God to us but it also reveals truth about ourselves and our position in relation to God. The Bible puts a name on the God-shaped hole within all of us and reveals our need for a Savior. It uncovers our spiritual bankruptcy and exposes our minds to the truth of the Gospel. The Bible should always be the first source and final judge of all "truth claims" we may encounter.

Chapter 3

<u>What Are Devotions?</u>

Coming back to my conversation with the lady I mentioned earlier, it occurred to me that some people are at a loss when it comes to devotions. This makes total sense because the word by itself doesn't fully convey its meaning. It's Christian shorthand, which is ok, but it is important to define what we mean by "devotions" as we move forward.

"Devotions" is a word used to describe the practice of regularly setting aside a specified amount of time to spend with God. This time almost always includes Bible reading and prayer but may also include meditation, reading of other materials, and writing. For our purposes we'll focus on three elements: Bible reading, prayer, and journaling.

Before we continue, let me just clarify that this book isn't intended to create a checklist for your devotional life. My intention is to kindle a spark of interest in a fulfilling, lifelong relationship with God. This isn't a devotional "how-to" or method book. My hope is that something you read will awaken a desire to know God and provide you with the basic tools necessary to do so.

The Four R's

So, let's look at some tools. Here are four elements of devotions that have been helpful to me in my spiritual life. They are: Read, Respond, Receive, and Record.

READ:

This stands for "reading" the Bible. This is the foundation of effective devotions. The Bible is literally God's Word. It was written down by faithful men under the inspiration of the Holy Spirit and remains relevant and effective to this day. Peter wrote,

"Above all, you must realize that no prophecy in Scripture ever came from the prophet's own understanding, or from human initiative. No, those prophets were moved by the Holy Spirit, and they spoke from God." (2 Peter 1:20–21 NLT)

Look at what Paul said to his spiritual son Timothy about the Scriptures,

"All Scripture is inspired by God and is useful to teach us what is true and to make us realize what is wrong in our lives. It corrects us when we are wrong and teaches us to do what is right. God uses it to prepare and equip his people to do every good work." (2 Timothy 3:16–17 NLT)

When we read the Bible we fuel ourselves with God's truth and reconnect to His purpose in us and for us. As Paul said, God uses it to prepare and equip his people! The Bible corrects us when we are wrong and teaches us to do what is right. It's our source and our standard. Maybe reading the Bible is difficult for you. I strongly encourage you to make it a discipline in your life. When you take that step it leads to God's word becoming a delight!

The Psalmist proclaimed,

> *"I will study your commandments and reflect on your ways. I will delight in your decrees and not forget your word. Be good to your servant, that I may live and obey your word. Open my eyes to see the wonderful truths in your instructions."* (Psalms 119:15–18 NLT)

And later in the same chapter,

> *"Oh, how I love your instructions! I think about them all day long...How sweet your words taste to me; they are sweeter than honey."* (Psalms 119:97, 103 NLT)

A daily discipline of Bible reading will soon become a delight to you but there's more. God's word can also become your defense.

Jesus responded to Satan's temptations in the wilderness three times with the words, "The Scriptures say..." or as it is recorded in another translation, "It is written..." Jesus Himself, the Son of God, depended on the truth and authority of the Scriptures to defend Himself! As followers of Jesus we should take the same posture of trust and dependence towards the Bible. The Scriptures are like a wall around us. They contain God's promise and His purpose for our lives.

Jesus said,

> *"Anyone who listens to my teaching and follows it is wise, like a person who builds a house on solid rock. Though the rain comes in torrents and the floodwaters rise and the winds beat against that house, it won't collapse because it is built on bedrock. But anyone who hears my teaching and doesn't obey it is foolish, like a person who builds a house on sand. When the rains and floods*

come and the winds beat against that house, it will collapse with a mighty crash." (Matthew 7:24–27 NLT)

RESPOND:

Successful devotions also include response. Response is a natural outflow of a healthy relationship and a healthy relationship with God is the goal of devotions. In my relationship with my wife one of the areas that I have tried to improve in is the area of responding. My wife doesn't feel valued or loved when I mutter monosyllabic sounds in her direction while staring at my phone when she's telling me something. Imagine that! Response is a critical part of relationships! The Bible tells us the story of a God who speaks and who listens. He's interested in our response.

The very act of God's creating humanity demonstrates God's desire to know and be known. Within the mystery of the Trinity there is community and communication and God chose to expand that fellowship to us! One of the most remarkable realities to reflect upon is that God made you and I for relationship with Him. It is incredible to me that the same God who set the planets in motion and cast the stars into the sky wants to talk to me and hear my voice in return.

So, how do we respond? First, we respond in worship. Worship is always a good idea! It's recognizing God for who He is and what He has done. It's responding in the most appropriate way possible because God is holy and worthy in every sense (and beyond) of these words.

Second, we can respond in prayer. Paul tells us,

> *"Don't worry about anything; instead, pray about everything. Tell God what you need, and thank him for all he has done."* (Philippians 4:6 NLT)

Prayer is the invited and even commanded response that we are to offer to God. More simply, prayer is communication with God. It is the lifeline to our Maker. In prayer we can pour out our hearts to God and hear His voice in return.

In prayer we can communicate and fellowship with God despite our imperfections because of the work of Jesus who is our High Priest. The writer of Hebrews tells us,

> *"So let us come boldly to the throne of our gracious God. There we will receive his mercy, and we will find grace to help us when we need it most."* (Hebrews 4:16 NLT)

So, be bold in your approach to God in prayer. That is not to say be prideful. Rather, we must come with the kind of bold humility that a child possesses when they approach their loving father. In prayer, we come not on the basis of our own righteousness but under the cover of Christ's atoning sacrifice.

RECEIVE:

Receiving is about hearing God through the

Scriptures and through prayer. God wants response but He's also responding. I once heard it said that "God is always speaking and we can hear Him if we'll listen." While I don't know if God is technically "always" speaking I do believe the principle is sound. Do I have a hearing ear and a receptive heart? Response is important but the goal of our devotions isn't to just fill the empty spaces with words.

Remember what Jesus said about prayer,

"When you pray, don't babble on and on as people of other religions do. They think their prayers are answered merely by repeating their words again and again. Don't be like them, for your Father knows exactly what you need even before you ask him!" (Matthew 6:7–8 NLT)

Receiving from God is just as important as responding. God knows our needs and our questions. Are we listening for His answer?

Beyond hearing God speak to us in prayer,

receiving also includes hearing God through the Scriptures. If a person tells me they are struggling to hear God I tell them to read their Bible. It isn't any less valuable than what He may speak directly to your heart. In fact, it's more valuable because it's infallible! The Bible must be the ultimate standard we judge our lives and even our hearing ear by. If someone thinks they heard God speak something to them that contradicts the clear teaching of the Bible than they should defer to the Bible. There is a wonderful safety and freedom in that simple trust.

Beyond that, we can receive knowledge, wisdom, and insight from the Bible to help us become the people that God created us to be. What we receive in our devotions is truly the Rocket Fuel that help us achieve new heights in our life of faith.

RECORD:

"Record" refers to simply writing down what you received and maybe even how you responded in your devotions. This step is simple but powerful. By recording what God speaks to you in your devotions you begin to create a testament to His love, faithfulness, and fulfilled promises. Over time you begin to create a record of your relationship with God.

I'm moved by the stories of elderly couples that keep the love letters written to each other throughout the years so that they can revisit them later. In the same way, when we record what God speaks to us in prayer and through the Scriptures it becomes a collection of letters from God that we can revisit for strength and encouragement in future moments. I can't tell you how many times I've gone back and read my devotional journal entries to remind myself of what God spoke to me or how He challenged me, etc.

This practice also has Biblical precedent. The ancient Israelites were instructed in this way,

"So commit yourselves wholeheartedly to these words of mine. Tie them to your hands and wear them on your forehead as reminders. Teach them to your children. Talk about them when you are at home and when you are on the road, when you are going to bed and when you are getting up. Write them on the doorposts of your house and on your gates, so that as long as the sky remains above the earth, you and your children may flourish in the land the LORD swore to give your ancestors. "Be careful to obey all these commands I am giving you. Show love to the LORD your God by walking in his ways and holding tightly to him." (Deuteronomy 11:18–22 NLT)

God's people are meant to keep a firm hold upon His Word and His commandments. We are meant to treasure the Word of God in our hearts and minds.

Look at what the Psalmist wrote here,

"I have hidden your word in my heart, that I might not sin against you." (Psalms 119:11 NLT)

In the next chapter we'll look at some practical methods for devotions and learn how to effectively read, respond, receive, and record.

To recap, we learned how to Read, Respond, Receive, and Record. Let me be clear about this method. It's just one of many methods that you might discover. The main point is to connect with God and that can look different for every person. But, as a general rule, the Bible and prayer should be the central focus of our devotions. God gave us the Bible for the purpose of revealing Himself and the message of salvation through Jesus. Prayer is literally communication with God! Without these two elements we are surely missing something important!

Jacob Schmelzer

Chapter 4

Strategies

Time and Place

To launch a rocket into space, certain conditions must be right. The weather is taken into consideration and so is the time of day. The location is also key. In the summer of 1950 a hybrid missile/rocket built from the pieces of a captured German V2 was launched from the east coast of Florida. The place was Cape Canaveral and it would become famous for the many launches that would take place there in the future. So what makes it special? It was chosen because its proximity to the equator and eastward orientation take advantage of the earth's spin and give rockets a boost. It's a rocket slingshot!

In the same way, time and place play a role in devotions. They can provide a "boost" in your spiritual life. Essentially, devotions are spending time with God. That's the important part. But, it's incredibly helpful to set aside a specific time and place to do so.

The Psalmist wrote about praising and singing to God in the morning and the evening.

> *"But as for me, I will sing about your power. Each morning I will sing with joy about your unfailing love. For you have been my refuge, a place of safety when I am in distress."* (Psalms 59:16 NLT) *"It is good to give thanks to the LORD, to sing praises to the Most High. It is good to proclaim your unfailing love in the morning, your faithfulness in the evening,* (Psalms 92:1–2 NLT)

In reality, there is no time that is technically better than any other when it comes to having your devotions. There is nothing magical about a particular time. Practically speaking though, first thing in the morning is often the best time because it allows you to meet with God before anything else happens. If you do nothing else that day at least you've connected with God!

I often practice a simple habit of opening my Bible and reading a few lines or even a whole chapter before getting out of bed. This small discipline helps get my heart and mind focused on God before any of the numerous (and normal) distractions of the day have a chance to grab my attention. It's so easy in this day and age of instant and constant connectivity to miss out on the rewarding experience of meeting with God.

Most followers of Christ who have built the discipline of daily devotions into their lives do them first thing in the morning. This doesn't mean that they all do but it's definitely a good idea. Start your day off right! So what about the place?

Where you do your devotions is not as

important as *why* you do them or *that* you do them but it does play a part. You want to pick a place that is relatively free from distractions and is comfortable enough for you to freely connect with God. Some people can have their devotions in a busy coffee shop while others need quiet and solitude. It just depends on your personality and temperament. Just find a place (or a few) that works and commit yourself to read, respond, receive, and record. Build a habit of daily devotions and reap the rewards!

The First Minute

If you're like me, you get easily distracted. It's hard for me to disconnect, sit still, and seek God. Sometimes I wish smart phones had never been invented! Do you know what I mean? What I've found is that the first minute of my devotions is the hardest. I suppose it's the same as running or lifting weights (not that I do those...). Anything that makes us stronger tends to start out tough.

The first minute is critical because it's where the battle is won or lost. Right when I sit down to read my Bible I'll think of something important I need to do that day. Distraction. Then I'll start craving food. Toast, where have you been all my life? Bananas! These things grow on trees? Wow! Distraction. My phone will magically seem like the most interesting thing in the world. Distraction! Do you ever feel this way?

Just pause. Take a breath. If you can stick with it, it will get easier. It's just our spoiled-rotten, over-indulged, under-challenged self trying to hide from what it needs. We need the Bible. We need prayer. We need God. Without Him we don't get off the ground.

If you can win the first minute it gets easier to win the second and the third and the fourth and so on. Try this. Open your Bible to where you're currently reading (do you have a reading plan?) and make eye contact with a spot somewhere on the next page. Mentally establish a goal to get there. Act like your life depends on it. It kind of does. I think you'll be surprised by what you can accomplish. Again, just win the first minute and see what happens next.

Portion Control

Oh those dreaded words! But, when it comes to losing weight they're golden. It's a simple fact. If you control your portions and take in less calories than you burn, you'll lose weight. So what? Well, portion control is important when it comes to devotions too. Obviously, more time with God is better right? Sure, but not at the expense of a regular time with Him. Repeat (preferably like a zombie) after me. Consistency is Key!

There's a reason most gyms are full in January and empty in March. People get excited to get in shape, make a commitment they can't keep, and quickly burn out. It's ridiculous to think that our couch sitting, TV watching, potato chip eating brains will suddenly be able to kick into gear just because we made a New Year's Resolution! What we need is systemic change, change from the inside out, and that doesn't come easily. It takes time and it's really tough. Changing habits is hard.

It's exactly the same when it comes to devotions. If you don't have a discipline of Bible reading, prayer, and journaling don't expect to go from zero to hero overnight. This is a mistake I've made over and over in my spiritual journey. It's easy to do when you love God and want to please Him. A few times I've gotten pumped up and promised myself that I was going to start praying and reading my Bible for 2 or 3 hours a day. I'm going to be a Christian Arnold Schwarzenegger with bulging spiritual muscles! Demons will tremble and flee at the mention of my name! Thousands of people will be saved when I spontaneously start preaching at the mall...

Two days later I'm lucky if I can finish a chapter of Matthew and a dinky little Psalm! No discipline and no habit equals no success. Devotions, like relationships, thrive on consistency. You're better off reading one verse and really letting it sink in than six chapters that fly right by you. Pastor Rick Warren once said, "It's not how much of God's Word you get through. It's how much of God's Word that gets through you." I love that statement because it takes away the excuse. I don't need to be great. I just need to show up. Do we trust God enough to start small? Do we have enough humility to admit that we're spiritual couch potatoes and enough courage to do something about it?

Resistance is Good

"But it's hard!"

"I just don't feel God like I used to."

"I'm just in a dry season right now."

"I'm not feeling it…"

Have you heard (or said) anything like the statements above? I know I have. This is usually how it goes with devotions. You get pumped up about doing your devotions and hit it hard for a few days. It feels great and then all of the sudden you wake up and the mojo is gone. That initial excitement and energy is nowhere to be found. You open your Bible but the words swim before your eyes and it feels like it takes you an hour to read a chapter. You try to pray but your mind is blank and your tongue stops working. You can't think of a single thing to pray about.

The next day you wake up and you're hoping the feeling is back...but it's not. Maybe a day off? Bye bye good habit. Two weeks later you realize you haven't cracked open your Bible or prayed in days. The guilt comes and you feel like a bad Christian.

Ok, stop right there. Let's go back and think about that day when it got hard. Did you know that's a good sign? Seriously. The fact that it got hard means you were making progress. Resistance leads to growth. Think about it in another way. When you want to build muscle you have to break it down through resistance. That's what weight lifting is all about. You strain and struggle against a heavy weight and it actually breaks your muscles down. Then, as you rest, your body uses nutrients to build the muscle back even stronger and what do you know, muscle growth! Resistance is good for us.

Now think about that day when your devotions got hard. You found the place of resistance. That's not the place to run from. It's the place to run to! When we encounter resistance in our spiritual disciplines it means they're working. We're breaking down that part of us that doesn't want God's will and allowing the Holy Spirit to replace it with His character and nature.

Resistance could also mean you're making a spiritual breakthrough and the enemy (aka

Satan) doesn't like it. He wants you comfortable and contained. Ever wonder why it's easy to sit still for two hours in a movie theater but torture to sit that long in church? I know, I know. Movies have more explosions than church but is that all it is? I'd wager that there's more to the story than meets the eye. We do have an enemy and when we feel resistance it could mean we're bumping up against his territory. Again, this is good! Keep fighting the good fight.

When the going gets tough don't get discouraged. Get excited! You're winning! Spiritual disciplines are no less challenging than physical ones. Devotions can be a lot like a workout. But, the results are even better! Paul told his disciple Timothy,

> *"Physical training is good, but training for godliness is much better, promising benefits in this life and in the life to come."* (1 Timothy 4:8 NLT)

Your discipline in devotions will benefit your life now and for eternity! That's worth it in my book. Push through the pain. If you do you will discover the amazing reward that is a relationship with Jesus. He is worth it. He's worth it all.

Chapter 5

How Do I Pray?

Remember the story from the beginning of the book about the lady who said she didn't know how to pray? This is a common issue for many Christians who have been taught that they should pray but don't know how. So, let's learn how to pray! And who better to teach us than Jesus Himself? Luke the physician, one of Jesus' followers recorded a story about Jesus disciples coming to Him with a request. It might seem familiar!

> *"1 Now Jesus was praying in a certain place, and when he finished, one of his disciples said to him, 'Lord, teach us to pray, as John taught his disciples.' 2 And he said to them, 'When you pray, say: 'Father, hallowed be your name. Your kingdom come.*

3 Give us each day our daily bread, 4 and forgive us our sins, for we ourselves forgive everyone who is indebted to us. And lead us not into temptation.'" (Luke 11:1–4 ESV)

If you've ever felt ashamed or discouraged about not knowing how to pray please don't! Even Jesus' own disciples had to ask Him how to pray. So, let's learn alongside of them shall we? Jesus' answer to their question is interesting because it is so simple. Jesus gave His disciples a simple prayer to pray. We know it as the Lord's prayer. This is a great foundation upon which to build your prayer life! It's even ok to simply repeat the words of the Lord's prayer exactly as Jesus spoke them as a prayer to God. Let's look into these wonderful words and see what they can teach us about relating to God in prayer.

First, the Lord's prayer begins with the Father and our relationship to Him.

"Father, hallowed be your name."

The Lord's prayer starts off with an acknowledgment that God is our Father. He's not just an impersonal cosmic force. He's our Father and He cares for us as a loving father does. He is interested in hearing our voice and spending time with us! Isn't that a wonderful thought? But it's true! You and I were created to know and be known. We were created for eternal relationship with God. We were created to worship and enjoy Him. So, we come to Him first as Father.

The prayer continues:

"...hallowed be Your name."

That word "hallowed" means "to honor as holy." This phrase is a statement of worship. We are declaring that God's name is holy, set apart from and above every other name. We are identifying the unique position of worth and power that our God occupies.

Take note of something powerful here! Our relationship with God in prayer should always begin with approaching God as our Father in an attitude of worship. The prayer doesn't start by dealing with our sin or our need for provision. It starts with God. Even in the Lord's Prayer there is a declaration of the Gospel! We can come to God our Father in worship because of what Jesus has done.

Matthew, one of Jesus twelve disciples records Jesus' prayer in slightly greater detail. Jesus said,

> *"9 Pray then like this: 'Our Father in heaven, hallowed be your name. 10 Your kingdom come, your will be done, on earth as it is in heaven. 11 Give us this day our daily bread, 12 and forgive us our debts, as we also have forgiven our debtors. 13 And lead us not into temptation, but deliver us from evil.'"* (Matthew 6:9–13 ESV)

After we acknowledge God as our Father and approach Him in worship we move to the next line in the prayer.

"Your kingdom come, Your will be done, on earth as it is in heaven."

This is a powerful phrase that can teach us much about the purpose of prayer. We are to seek the establishment of God's kingdom here on earth. As followers of Jesus we look forward with hopeful expectation to eternity with Him but Jesus invites us to experience the fruits of eternity here and now. As Dallas Willard said, "Eternity is now in session. We can enter the eternal kind of life now." This portion of the Lord's Prayer focuses our attention on this reality.

We are to pray that this world would begin to reflect what God's kingdom looks like. We are to seek that His will would be done and His Kingdom established in our communities, families and in ourselves! And, the good news is that if Jesus included this in the prayer it is indeed a possibility. In other words, we can be a part of seeing the world around us look more like God's kingdom. God wants to move in and through us to change the world for the better.

Jesus continues,

> *"Give us this day our daily bread, and forgive us our debts as we also have forgiven our debtors."*

Jesus demonstrates to us how to pray for our practical and spiritual needs. We are to depend upon Jesus for daily provision of bread (our practical needs) and also forgiveness. Note here that our forgiveness is also contingent upon our forgiving of others. We can't expect God's forgiveness to flow *to* us if we won't allow it to flow *through* us.

Most people's prayer life centers around these topics but Jesus put them farther down the list when He taught His disciples how to pray. We often begin our prayers by asking God to forgive us and then start asking for stuff but that's out of order! I think we often start our prayers feeling guilty and so we look for a quick conscience cleanse. I always used to pray this way. First thing in the morning when I started to pray my thoughts would drift to all the things that I'd done wrong the day before. I'd feel guilty and unworthy to approach God so I'd always start by asking for forgiveness. Now, there's nothing wrong with asking God to forgive you of your sin but Jesus demonstrates a better way.

When we approach God in guilt we demonstrate a lack of belief in the effective power of the Gospel. The good news of what Jesus has done for us is that He has reconciled us to God. Paul explains this wonderful reality in his letter to the Romans,

> *"10 For since our friendship with God was restored by the death of his Son while we were still his enemies, we will certainly be saved through the life of his Son. 11 So now we can rejoice in our wonderful new relationship with God because our Lord Jesus Christ has made us friends of God."* (Romans 5:10–11 NLT)

We can rejoice in "our wonderful new relationship with God because our Lord Jesus Christ has made us friends of God!" Let those words sink into your heart as we think about prayer. If prayer is communication with God, and you have been given a wonderful new relationship with Him, you can enjoy it! Paul tells us that through Jesus we have been made friends of God. The message of the Gospel is true. If you've put your faith and trust in Jesus Christ you now have access to God. So, don't come in guilt or shame. Come as a friend.

This doesn't mean that we don't need to ask for forgiveness. Jesus included it in the prayer. But, I find it interesting that He didn't give it a preeminent place as we often do. The order of the Lord's prayer is a reflection of the Gospel which prioritizes a relationship with God.

So, what about daily bread? This part of the prayer emphasizes our need to depend upon God for our practical needs. This might have seemed more relevant to Jesus' disciples who were not affluent men but it's just as important to us. If you live in an affluent society it is incredibly easy to stop depending upon God for provision. Jesus reminds us not to do that! This doesn't mean that we can't be prosperous and blessed but rather that we are always to acknowledge our source! And, we are to remain open-handed and humble with regards to our possessions. Possess your possessions. Don't let them possess you. Depend on God daily.

In the same way that we're tempted to approach God from a place of guilt we can be tempted to approach God from a place of need. But, Jesus didn't prioritize this either. God cares about our needs but they're not supposed to be the foundation of our relationship. Some Christians treat prayer like a spiritual vending machine. That's not what Jesus taught. He told His disciples to ask for daily bread, not a lifetime supply. God knows that our hearts crave the prideful certainty of self-dependence but He's merciful enough to keep us from it!

Jacob Schmelzer

When we pray for daily bread and live a life of trust it keeps us safe in the hands of God.

Paul offers a thought about prayer,

> *"6 Don't worry about anything; instead, pray about everything. Tell God what you need, and thank him for all he has done. 7 Then you will experience God's peace, which exceeds anything we can understand. His peace will guard your hearts and minds as you live in Christ Jesus."* (Philippians 4:6–7 NLT)

When we depend upon God for our practical needs we can have the peace that Paul is talking about! Peace is the prize that our hearts want when we seek to be self-dependent but it will never be found there. It is only found in a trust based relationship with God.

Finally, Jesus finishes His prayer with the phrase,

> *"And lead us not into temptation, but deliver us from evil."*

To clarify, Jesus isn't indicating that God does sometimes lead us into tempting situations. The aim here is that temptation exists and Jesus' followers should ask God to help them avoid and escape it! This line in the prayer draws our focus to the reality of the fallen world we live in. It calls us to attention and alert. There is a danger of falling into tempting situations and an active evil that opposes us. The Lord's Prayer isn't just soft and fluffy! Jesus instructs His disciples to seek God's leading and protection in a perilous world.

The Lord's prayer is the perfect foundation of our prayer life. It was and is Jesus' lesson on what prayer is to be. I'll some it up briefly in four words that can help us remember how to pray through it. First, comes **WORSHIP**. We approach God our Father in reverence and honor. Second, comes **WILL**. We ask God to establish His kingdom in and around us. Third, comes **WELFARE**. We ask God for daily provision and forgiveness of our sins. Fourth, comes **WARFARE**. We ask God to lead and protect us as we follow Jesus.

Hopefully these four words (WORSHIP, WILL, WELFARE, and WARFARE) will help you to simply and effectively pray through the Lord's prayer. Remember, its fine to just repeat the words of the Lord's prayer! I believe that if you will honor and obey God by beginning to pray through the Lord's prayer He will open up a rich and satisfying prayer life to you that can endure for a lifetime!

Chapter 6

<u>Retreat to Advance</u>

One of the greatest lessons Jesus demonstrated to His followers was how to retreat to advance. Jesus would often withdraw Himself from His disciples and followers to be alone and pray. In our world of near-total connectivity and productivity obsession we can easily miss this critical discipline. Luke gives us an insight into Jesus' personal practice:

> *"15 But despite Jesus' instructions, the report of his power spread even faster, and vast crowds came to hear him preach and to be healed of their diseases. 16 But Jesus often withdrew to the wilderness for prayer."* (Luke 5:15, 16 NLT)

Let's look at a couple of key things from what Luke said about Jesus. First off, Jesus had a powerful ministry. Vast crowds wanted to hear Him speak. People heard of His power and ability to heal the sick despite His efforts to keep it quiet. Jesus was in high demand! But look at what Luke says in verse 16, "But Jesus often withdrew to the wilderness for prayer." Jesus OFTEN withdrew for prayer. How many of us, if we had the power and effectiveness of Jesus, would want to keep it quiet and then often go hide out in the wilderness? Not me. Heck no!

If I had Jesus' power and influence I'd want to use it all the time and for the benefit of as many people as possible! So what's up with Jesus? Well, Jesus understood a secret that we often miss. His success came from His relationship with God. The source of His power was in His secret time with His father. Now, you might be thinking, "Well isn't Jesus God?" Yes, that's correct but Paul tells us in Philippians 2 that Jesus emptied Himself of

His divine attributes:

> "6 Though he was God, he did not think of equality with God as something to cling to. 7 Instead, he gave up his divine privileges; he took the humble position of a slave and was born as a human being. When he appeared in human form, 8 he humbled himself in obedience to God and died a criminal's death on a cross." (Philippians 2:6–8 NLT)

Jesus became a human being like us and had to depend upon God in the same way that we do. Jesus didn't just come to die on the cross for our sins! He also lived to teach us how to live. Here in Luke 5 we get a glimpse of what Jesus prioritized. He didn't prioritize the display of His power. He prioritized the place of prayer! Do we?

Have we learned to disconnect from the world around us and get alone with God? If Jesus needed it so do we! Often, the best way to advance is to retreat to the secret place of prayer. A daily discipline of devotions keeps you fresh and connected to God. Retreat to advance.

What does this look like practically? First, it means disconnecting from the world around you. It's about removing yourself from all demands on your attention. This could look like shutting off your phone or leaving it in another room. It might mean leaving your house to go for a walk. It could be setting up a unique space in your house for your prayer time. Remember that Jesus would literally go into the wilderness! He separated Himself from His friends and His followers to be alone with God. We need to do the same.

Second, we have to create space for our heart and mind to be able to hear God's voice. We live in a world of total connectivity and constant noise. When's the last time you were in a totally silent environment and could hear yourself think? Most of us are unaccustomed to this. We are used to being connected and wrapped in our sensory perceptions. So, once we separate ourselves from distractions and other people we need to prepare our souls to connect with God. This might mean quietly meditating on a passage of Scripture or softly praying. The idea is to slow down our thoughts, which are normally moving a million miles an hour, to the speed of peace.

I love the story in the book of 1 Kings about the prophet Elijah. He was hiding out in a cave on Mount Sinai and God came to speak with him:

> "11 *"Go out and stand before me on the mountain," the Lord told him. And as Elijah stood there, the Lord passed by, and a mighty windstorm hit the mountain. It was such a terrible blast that the rocks were torn loose, but the Lord was not in the wind. After the wind there was an earthquake, but the Lord was not in the earthquake. 12 And after the earthquake there was a fire, but the*

Lord was not in the fire. And after the fire there was the sound of a gentle whisper. 13 When Elijah heard it, he wrapped his face in his cloak and went out and stood at the entrance of the cave. And a voice said, "What are you doing here, Elijah?" (1 Kings 19:11–13 NLT)

In the account, God wasn't in the whirlwind, or the earthquake, or the fire! He was in the gentle whisper. So, think about your time with God. Is your soul quiet enough to hear God's whisper? Creating space is vital to our prayer life!

David was a man who depended upon God and he spoke of this in his psalms:

"1 I wait quietly before God, for my victory comes from him...5 Let all that I am wait quietly before God, for my hope is in him." (Psalms 62:1, 5 NLT)

"1 Lord, my heart is not proud; my eyes are not haughty. I don't concern myself

with matters too great or too awesome for me to grasp. 2 Instead, I have calmed and quieted myself, like a weaned child who no longer cries for its mother's milk. Yes, like a weaned child is my soul within me." (Psalms 131:1, 2 NLT)

Jesus demonstrated these great disciplines of separating from distraction and creating space. But, there is another key to be found in Luke's account. It's the word *often.* Jesus OFTEN withdrew to pray. For Jesus, prayer was a critical habit and a lifestyle. Jesus prayer life wasn't based on circumstance. It was based on relationship. Many of us treat God like a vending machine when we only pray or spend time with Him on the basis of a current need. It's ok to pray for our needs but that's only a small part of an incredibly rich relationship that we can enjoy with God. When we learn to have a lifestyle of prayer and time with God we will begin to experience life as God intended it to be lived.

If we look back to the Garden of Eden before the fall of mankind we see a picture of a life full of communion and relationship with God the creator. Adam and Eve enjoyed a rich relationship with God that was unstained by sin! This relationship has been opened up for us again through Jesus Christ but we often neglect it. Let's follow Jesus' example instead and OFTEN go to the place of prayer.

Chapter 7

The Power of Devotions

I'm a practical person. I like to know what I'm supposed to get out of something if I give my time and energy to it! I've found that investing my time and energy into daily devotions to build my relationship with God has been enormously rewarding to me and I highly recommend it! Here's three benefits that I've observed in my life as a result of my devotional life.

First, when I consistently spend time in devotions I notice that my emotions and moods are much better! I'm generally more joyful and it's not connected to my external circumstances. When I'm consistently meeting with God I get a more eternal perspective and the ups and downs of my day to day life don't affect me as much.

This doesn't mean that I never get tired or bummed out, because I do. But I definitely notice that my peace and contentment factor goes way up regardless of what's going on. I'd call this the joy factor!

Second, when I consistently meet with God my relationship with Him gets better. What a concept, right? Seriously though, consistent time with God makes me more sensitive to His voice and His leading in my life. I feel His presence more often and actually desire it more as well. This leads to a greater sense of peace and integration in my life. I feel connected to my Creator and more in tune with my life purpose!

Third, my appetite for sin is diminished and my capacity for good is increased. Internal transformation begins to take place! This one is interesting because for a long time I approached my own weaknesses from a perspective of needing to do better to be accepted. That's an anti-gospel perspective and it really messed up my devotional life. I felt unworthy to enjoy fellowship with God and turned my prayers into constant apologies and my Bible reading into penance. I was missing the point completely! We don't do right for God so we can have a relationship with Him. We have a relationship with God that allows us to do right. I was getting it backwards. Now, I understand that I'm accepted because of what Jesus did and now I can freely perform righteously because of my relationship with God.

I could never earn the right to have a relationship with God. Jesus did that on my behalf and now I can enter into God's presence. My devotional life no longer rides an emotional roller coaster based on my good or bad behavior. I understand that I need Jesus just as much every day! He's my righteousness and it's through my relationship with Him that I am sanctified.

Paul says it this way,

"21 For He made Him who knew no sin to be sin for us, that we might become the righteousness of God in Him." (2 Corinthians 5:21 NKJV)

We become the righteousness of God in Christ! What an amazing truth! Believing this truth will transform your devotional life into something powerful. Instead of hiding from God when we fail we should come running!

Paul spoke about these realities in his letter to the Romans,

"17 for the kingdom of God is not eating and drinking, but righteousness and peace and joy in the Holy Spirit." (Romans 14:17 NKJV)

The kingdom of God is righteousness, peace, and joy in the Holy Spirit! Because of what Jesus did for us we can access God's presence on a daily basis and walk in righteousness, peace, and joy! This is what is on offer through a relationship with Jesus.

We don't have to wait until we get to heaven to experience God's kingdom. In fact, we are invited to be conduits through which God's kingdom can be established on earth right now. Remember the second line of Jesus' prayer? Jesus told His disciples to pray these words, "Your kingdom come, Your will be done, on earth as it is in heaven." We should be seeking God's kingdom here and now both for ourselves and the world around us. By connecting with God in devotions we can experience the fruits of the Kingdom which are righteousness, peace, and joy in the Holy Spirit.

God has invited us to become living representations of what His kingdom looks like. The world around us might be evil, in chaos, and filled with despair but we will be bringing in righteousness, peace, and joy wherever we go! What better proclamation of the gospel can you have than a follower of Jesus who is representing the kingdom of God like this?

People were drawn to Jesus because He lived out God's kingdom and people should be drawn to us for the same reason.

Chapter 8

The Plan

So where do we start? Where's the Rocket Fuel? What's the plan? Honestly, the best plan is the one you start right now. General George S. Patton, a salty WWII general, famously said, "A good plan, violently executed now, is better than a perfect plan next week." I love that quote and it fits perfectly when it comes to devotions. They're exactly like a war. We're fighting an enemy (in this case ourselves and the devil) and the best strategy is to simply attack. Instead of being hung up on a lack of knowledge or insecurity in our methodology let's just move forward. Just Read, Respond, Receive, and Record. Then repeat. Beat back the enemy. Take the ground you've been assigned to take and then hold on. It's not rocket science.

When you kick into action with your devotions you just get stronger. It's an incredible thing. When we seek God we find Him! He reveals Himself more and more and we are changed and transformed from the inside out. He's the fuel and He's the fire. As we pour ourselves out He fills us up and we're never the same! Our relationship with Christ breaks us out of the atmosphere of our own self-centeredness and shows us an amazing view of what God intended all along.

Practically speaking, all you need is a simple plan that you can start now. First, I'd encourage you to get a Bible reading plan that you can realistically commit yourself to do. There are lots of free ones online that are great! Some of them have you read the entire Bible in one year and others break it up over a longer period of time. It's up to you how much you can commit yourself to read but I'd encourage consistent quality time over quantity. You want the Scriptures to really go deep so don't overreach in an effort to achieve something. If you read, you win. It's that simple.

There is a mobile app called YouVersion for tablets and smart phones that has a bunch of free Bible reading plans, devotionals, and even different translations. It's a great way to have your Bible always with you! But, it can be a distraction to have your phone double as your Bible when you're getting texts and Facebook notifications while you're trying to read!

Second, set aside a few minutes to pray and start with a guide. I really encourage you to learn how to pray through the Lord's Prayer which I go through at length in this book. It's an incredible foundation for learning how to pray and it never gets old! It just becomes more meaningful as you go.

Third, get yourself a cool journal that you can write down what God speaks to you in. I remember my first (cool) prayer journal with a leather cover and sweet gold letter dove emblazoned on the front! I still have it! It's so great to go back and read through the things that God was speaking to me all those years ago. In your journal it's helpful to write Scriptures that God opens up to you, your own thoughts and insights, and even to write out your prayers. Sometimes, I'll write out an entire prayer and I enjoy that because it helps me slow down enough to really think through what I am saying to God.

Here's an example of an easy, three-step plan that you can put into action right away. With our youth group we did a series called the "15 Challenge" where we encouraged our students to spend fifteen minutes with God each day. The fifteen minutes were broken up into three five minute segments: Bible reading, prayer, and journaling. It was a great experience and I loved the simplicity of it. Everyone has at least fifteen minutes that they can give to God! It's not much but it can be the start of an incredibly valuable habit of daily devotions.

Chapter 9

In Orbit

I've always enjoyed looking at pictures of the earth taken from space. It's amazing to think of how few human beings have had an opportunity to go to outer space and look back at our planet! In the same way, it's interesting that so few people really achieve the heights of relationship with God that they could. I'm one of them. Even though I know what Jesus has provided for me I often miss out for a variety of reasons. Sometimes its busyness. Sometimes its distraction. Sometimes it's my own sense of unworthiness. But, I am so thankful that despite my wandering heart God is always faithful to me! He's waiting for me in the place of prayer and devotion. He's my Father and He delights in my company.

The truth is that no matter how much I might feel love for Him, His love is always greater for me! And, that's the truth that always draws me back! It's the truth that calls to my soul even when I'm distracted, depressed, or disconnected. It's the gentle whisper that calls me to pull away from the world for a few moments to meet with my Father. Let me leave you with this. Devotions are not a ladder that we climb to God. If you approach them with that mindset you'll miss out on the amazing relationship that God wants to have with you! As Dallas Willard said, "Spiritual disciplines aren't righteousness, they're wisdom." Having a disciplined devotional life is immensely rewarding to every follower of Jesus but it doesn't make us more acceptable to God. Only, the work of Christ at Calvary could do that! We don't approach to be accepted. We approach because we've already been accepted!

When we connect with this truth and allow it to take root in our hearts our devotional life will never be the same. We will approach God in joyful worship with a heart for a real relationship. This is what God is after! He's looking for sons and daughters who will come to Him of their own freewill and love.

Look at what Paul says in Romans 8,

> *"15 So you have not received a spirit that makes you fearful slaves. Instead, you received God's Spirit when he adopted you as his own children. Now we call him, "Abba, Father." 16 For his Spirit joins with our spirit to affirm that we are God's children. 17 And since we are his children, we are his heirs. In fact, together with Christ we are heirs of God's glory. But if we are to share his glory, we must also share his suffering. 18 Yet what we suffer now is nothing compared to the glory he will reveal to us later. 19 For all creation is waiting eagerly for that future day when God will reveal who his children really are."* (Romans 8:15–19 NLT)

We are the children of God! We are His heirs and all creation eagerly awaits the unveiling of who God's children really are. Even though we will go through suffering it will be worth it. Paul tells us that we didn't "receive a spirit that makes us fearful slaves." We have been adopted into God's family. Look at what Keith Green wrote about this topic in His journal,

> "Do You remember how it was when you first met Jesus? Do you remember how you delighted to call God your 'Daddy,' your 'Abba, Father'? You enjoyed the intimacy of a child with its papa. And now how is it? Is He still "Daddy" or has He become 'Reverend Holy Father'? Has the intimacy been replaced with a formalism that keeps Him at arm's length?"

> Keith continues, "Grow in Christ but never lose the childlike spirit that cries out boldly, 'Abba, Father.'"

If you're going to enter spiritual orbit you have to keep this simple truth in mind! It's about what Jesus has done not what we can do. God wants to have a relationship with you and He made a way for it to happen through Jesus! Again, our devotional life isn't something we achieve in the sense of winning a prize or reaching a certain level. It's a place of fellowship that we have been invited into. We come to Abba Father in simple love and humility and receive all that we need!

To really take flight and break into orbit we must give up our own efforts toward God and embrace His efforts toward us. The secret is in allowing God to fill us with Himself! That's the real Rocket Fuel. It's the power of a life that has been emptied of self and filled with God. It's a paradox that we are empty when we are full and full when we are empty!

John the Baptist said of Jesus,

> *"30 He must increase, but I must decrease."* (John 3:30 NKJV)

Our effort should be directed at making room for God to fill us! That should be our posture towards Him. Paul talked about a "thorn in the flesh" that he desperately wanted to be delivered from but take a look at God's response,

> *"8 Three different times I begged the Lord to take it away. 9 Each time he said, "My grace is all you need. My power works best in weakness." So now I am glad to boast about my weaknesses, so that the power of Christ can work through me. 10 That's why I take pleasure in my weaknesses, and in the insults, hardships, persecutions, and troubles that I suffer for Christ. For when I am weak, then I am strong."* (2 Corinthians 12:8-10 NLT)

This doesn't sound fun but there's a deep truth to be found here. God's glory is more clearly seen in our weakness! When we are weak He is strong! Let's apply this to the area of devotions. I don't want to convey that the discipline of devotions makes us "better" or "more acceptable" in the eyes of God. Dead religion turns devotions into a penance through which we make ourselves better. Again, they aren't a ladder by which we climb up to God. They are a place that God has provided us to meet with Him. If anyone is climbing a ladder it's God climbing down to our level! When we get that right in our minds we learn to fly.

It's the paradox of how God's kingdom works. In God's kingdom the greatest are servants and the humble are exalted! In God's kingdom the King has come down to the subjects and made them royalty. Therefore, humility is key when it comes to relating to God. Peter speaks of this,

> *"...God opposes the proud but gives grace to the humble." 6 So humble yourselves under the mighty power of God, and at the right time he will lift you up in honor. 7 Give all your worries and cares to God,*

for he cares about you." (1 Peter 5:5b–7 NLT)

Peter clues us in to how God deals with our attitude. He gives grace to the humble but He opposes the proud! There is a warning here. Don't ever get proud about your level of devotion to God. Humbly accept God's devotion to you and allow that truth to soak your heart with grace. A grace soaked heart can only approach God with bold humility! A true son or daughter of God enjoys their place in the presence of God but doesn't think that their own efforts got them there!

It's my prayer that something you read in this book will stir your heart to seek God fresh and new. Maybe you attempted to have a regular time with God but stopped for some reason. Or maybe you've never even started. Wherever you're at right now I encourage you to try again! Other than putting your trust in Jesus I can't think of a better choice you could make.

Spending time in the presence of God is the natural outflow of our salvation. It's one of the primary benefits that Jesus opened up to us. So, I challenge you to set aside some time right now to begin meeting regularly with God in your devotions. Let God become the fuel to your fire and see what incredible things He has in store for you!

Jacob Schmelzer

Connect with Jacob at:

www.jacobschmelzer.com

www.facebook.com/jacobschmelzermusic

www.ingramcontent.com/pod-product-compliance
Lightning Source LLC
Chambersburg PA
CBHW031630040426
42452CB00007B/761